ISBN: 978-1-912484-14-0
Published by Angelis Publications
www.angelispublications.com

A Year to Remember

Wishing You All A Happy New Year!
Wishing You All A Happy New Year!
Wishing You All A Happy New Year!
Wishing You All A Happy New Year!

Guests

Guests

Guests

Guests

Guests

Guests

Guests

Guests

Guests

Guests

Guests

Guests

Guests

Guests

Guests

Guests

Guests

Guests

Guests

Guests

Guests

Guests

Guests

Guests

Guests

Guests

Guests

Guests

Guests

Guests

Guests

Guests

Guests

Guests

Guests

Guests

Guests

Guests

Guests

Guests

Guests

Guests

Guests

Guests

Guests

Guests

Guests

Guests

Guests

Guests

Guests

Guests

Guests

Guests

Guests

Guests

Guests

Guests

Guests

Guests

Guests

Guests

Guests

Guests

Guests

Guests

Guests

Guests

Guests

Guests

Guests

Guests

Guests

Guests

Guests

Guests

Guests

Guests

Guests

Guests

Guests

Guests

Guests

Guests

Guests

Guests

Guests

Guests

Guests

Guests

Guests

Guests

Guests

Guests

Guests

www.ingramcontent.com/pod-product-compliance
Lightning Source LLC
Chambersburg PA
CBHW081126300726
48982CB00005B/865